Spaghetti, Again?

Spaghetti, Again?

A BEGINNING READER IN ENGLISH

Jean W. Bodman

Judith B. McKoy

COLLIER
MACMILLAN

Library of Congress Cataloging-in-Publication Data

Bodman, Jean.
    Spaghetti, again?

    1. English language—Text-books for foreign speakers.
2. Readers—   I. Title.
PE1128.B598 1988   428.6'4   86-31170
    ISBN 0-02-311590-4

Collier Macmillan Canada, Inc.

Cover and design: Anna Veltfort
Illustrations: Shelley Matheis

First printing 1988

Printing: 1 2 3 4 5 6 7   Year: 8 9 0 1 2 3 4

Collier Macmillan
866 Third Avenue
New York, NY 10022

Printed in the U.S.A.

ISBN 0-02-311590-4

Introduction

The Audience

Spaghetti, Again? is a high interest reader designed for adolescent and adult learners of English. It is also appropriate as a supplemental text for native English speakers in developmental reading programs.

The Level of the Book

Spaghetti, Again? is written for beginning learners of English and low-level adult basic education students in reading programs. The grammar, vocabulary, and concepts in the book are carefully controlled so that even the most elementary learners are able to read fluently. *Spaghetti, Again?* begins with readings that contain only the present tense of the verb *be* and a small number of other elementary grammatical structures; as the book progresses, other tenses and grammatical structures are introduced. (See pages 89–91 for a complete listing by chapter.) When unfamiliar concepts are introduced, students have a chance to discuss them before they read. Vocabulary is controlled and recycled throughout the book. (See pages 92–96.)

The Theory Behind the Book

Spaghetti, Again? is based on a widely accepted theory of reading called *schema theory*. According to schema theory, reading is seen as a dynamic, interactive process (not as a "passive" skill, as some have described it). Schema theory states that accurate comprehension of a text is dependent on the prior knowledge that readers bring to the reading activity or the concepts they are able to activate by reading the text. The readers arrange these concepts in their minds to form a schema (a tentative interpretation of the text).

For example, when readers are presented with this sentence:

> *After they were pronounced husband and wife, the couple was congratulated by their friends and relatives.*

a number of concepts are activated. Most English-speaking readers "see" a minister, a bride, a groom, and some other people shaking hands and kissing the couple. Many readers go even further—they see a church, a bride in a white gown, a groom in a tuxedo, bridesmaids, and other people formally dressed. In any event, almost all readers infer that this sentence is from a story about a wedding even though this is not explicitly stated.

When presented with the next sentence:

> *Then the food was brought into the living room where everyone was standing, and Father Murphy made the first toast.*

some of the concepts in the first interpretation would be confirmed while others would have to be revised. For example, the concept "church" would have to be eliminated and replaced with the concept "private home." Thus, the new interpretation of the story is: a man and a woman have just been married in someone's living room. This interpretation then becomes the frame of reference for additional information as it is read. Interpretations, therefore, are not static; they are modified or altered whenever additional data makes this necessary.

The interpretation provides the basis for all higher-level reasoning tasks. Good readers not only develop an accurate interpretation of the text by using the concepts activated by the text, their knowledge of the world, and their knowledge of English, but they also formulate questions as they read: what's this story about? why did that happen? what's going to happen next? The questions, the interpretation, and the readers' prior knowledge help readers make inferences, anticipate outcomes, speculate, and compare and contrast previously held information with new information, make generalizations, and so on. Good readers do not wait until they have finished reading to start thinking about the text. They activate their thinking skills immediately.

The Organization of the Book

Since we would like all of our learners to read the way that good readers do, *Spaghetti, Again?* attempts to ensure that all readers have sufficient knowledge of the concepts and vocabulary needed to comprehend the text before they begin to read. The illustrations that begin each chapter, in the *Developing New Concepts and Vocabulary* section, are designed to trigger or activate the schema the readers need to interpret the story accurately.

In the *Thinking and Questioning* section, readers are shown illustrations pertinent to the main story line and are directed to make at least one question. Thus readers are taught to view reading as an active, thinking process.

In the *Comprehension Activities* section, readers complete exercises that test their interpretive and inferential reasoning skills. This will encourage them to read beyond the literal level.

Vocabulary Practice serves to give the readers a chance to work with useful and important vocabulary from the story.

Comparing Old and New Concepts encourages students to discuss concepts from the story and to see reading as one way of learning about the world outside of one's own experience.

The Content

Spaghetti, Again? is set in the suburbs of a small Pennsylvania town. The story centers around the Lewis family, Sarah Lewis and her three children, and their complex lives. We have attempted to make the people in our story multidimensional. At one moment, they are warm, amusing, and compassionate; and the next moment, they are confused, worried, jealous, and temperamental. We have tried to present characters who are thoroughly human, who have real problems, which they solve in a variety of ways—some reasonable and some unreasonable. The readers are encouraged to use their own knowledge to discuss the issues raised in the book.

Jean W. Bodman
Judith B. McKoy

Acknowledgments

We are not alone. We are the sum of many intertwining lives. Our heartfelt thanks to Walter Karkosza and our families for their loving support; to Mary Jane Peluso and Karen Peratt for believing in this project; to John Lawrence for inspiration and encouragement; and to Pamela Breyer and Miriam Eisenstein for invaluable help with the manuscript. We are lucky in our friends.

Contents

Chapter

Spaghetti, Again?

Getting Ready to Read

1. Developing New Concepts and Vocabulary

A. Study Pictures 1, 2, 3, and 4 and the new words and phrases.

PICTURE 1

map
name
state

phrase
the United States

PICTURE 2

town
small
building

phrase
gas station

1

PICTURE 3

store   restaurant   man/men

church   car   woman/women

PICTURE 4

house   old   lawn

large   neat   paper

B. Say something about Pictures 1, 2, 3, and 4. Use the new words and phrases.

2

2. Thinking and Questioning

A. Study this picture and the new words and phrases.

dark	asleep	<u>phrases</u>
people	light	be on
		5:00 A.M.

B. Say something about the picture. Use the new words and phrases.

C. Think about the picture. Do you have any questions? Write two here:

1. Why _____ ?
2. Who _____ ?

Reading

Study these new words and phrases. Then read the story.

awake	empty	silent	<u>phrases</u>
cool	green	white	be around
different	quiet	window	be closed
			in the center of

Different

It is quiet, very quiet. No one is around. The stores are closed. The old, white church in the center of town is silent. The buildings are empty and dark. It is 5:00 A.M. in Madison, Pennsylvania.

Greenwood Street is cool and dark. The old, white houses with neat, green lawns are silent. Their windows are dark.

But one house on Greenwood Street is different. It is small, and the lawn is not very neat. There is a light on in the house. It is 5:00 A.M. Sarah Lewis is awake.

Comprehension Activities

1. Reviewing the Story

A. Write two things you know about Sarah Lewis.

1. _____

2. _____

B. Write two things you know about Madison, Pennsylvania.

1. _____

2. _____

C. The title of the story is "Different." What is "different" in the story? Name two things.

1. _____

2. _____

2. Wondering About the Story

Think about the story. What do you want to know? Write a question here:

_____ ?

Vocabulary Practice

A. Look at the pictures. Then finish the sentences. Use these words:

lawn   house   light   quiet   asleep   dark

PICTURE 1

This is a _____ .

PICTURE 2

There is some paper on the

_____ .

PICTURE 3

This room is _____ .

PICTURE 4

Now the _____ is on.

PICTURE 5

The woman is _____ .

PICTURE 6

It's 2:00 A.M. Greenwood Street is

_____ .

B. Complete this exercise. Use vocabulary from the story.

1. Name something that is green.

    (For example: A car is green.)

    _____

2. Name something that is white.

    _____

3. Name a kind of building.

    (For example: A store is a building.)

    _____

Comparing Old and New Concepts

1. Think about a town, street, or house that you know.
   Is it different from the pictures on pages 1 and 2?
   How is it different?

2. Sarah is awake at 5:00 A.M. Think about the people that you know.
   Are they awake or asleep at 5:00 A.M.?

MORE DIFFICULT QUESTIONS

Many Americans think it is very important to have a neat and beautiful lawn in front of their house.
Do you think that is important?
Is what your neighbors think of you important?

Chapter

2

Getting Ready to Read

1. Developing New Concepts and Vocabulary

A. Study these pictures and the new words and phrases.

PICTURE 1

child/children

mother

daughter

son

girl

boy

<u>phrase</u>

_____ years old

PICTURE 2

book

bed

clothes

room

bedroom

<u>phrase</u>

be all over

B. Say something about Pictures 1 and 2. Use the new words and phrases.

2. Thinking and Questioning

A. Study these pictures and the new words.

PICTURE 1

kitchen

morning

call (to)

PICTURE 2

knock (on)

door

B. Say something about the two pictures. Use the new words.

C. Think about these pictures. Do you have any questions? Write two here:

1. Where _____ ?

2. Why _____ ?

Reading

Study these new words. Then read the story.

answer   early   still   usually

⚠ dummy   maybe   today

Where Is She?

Sarah Lewis is thirty-nine years old. She is the mother of two girls, Tina and Carol, and a boy, Ben. Early in the morning, when it is quiet and her children are asleep, Sarah's light is on. Her bedroom is not very neat. There are books all over her bed, all over the room.

It is 7:30 A.M. The children are awake. Their mother is usually in the kitchen at 7:30, but today she is not there.

Tina: Where's Mom?
Carol: What?
Tina: Mom. Where is she?
Ben: She's in the kitchen, dummy.
Tina: No, she isn't.
Carol: She isn't?
Tina: No. Where is she?
Ben: Maybe she's still in her room.
Tina: Maybe. Her door's closed.

Tina knocks on her mother's door and calls to her.

Tina: Mom!

There is no answer.

Tina: MOM!

There is still no answer.

Tina: *MO-THER!*
Carol: Is she there?

Note: Reading Punctuation and Italics

Read the following words out loud. Say each one differently.

Mom.   Mom!   MOM!   *MO-THER!*

Comprehension Activities

1. Reviewing the Story

A. Write three things you know about Sarah Lewis and her children.

1. _____
   _____

2. _____
   _____

3. _____
   _____

B. Finish the following sentences.

1. Sarah's bedroom is not very neat because _____
   _____ .

2. Tina knocks on her mother's door because _____
   _____ .

2. Wondering About the Story

Think about the story. What do you want to know? Write a question here:

_____ ?

3. Making a Guess

Where do you think Sarah, their mother, is? Circle one picture.

Vocabulary Practice

A. Look at the pictures. Then finish the sentences. Use these words:

boy   girl   morning   children

PICTURE 1

This is Sarah Lewis and her three

_____ .

PICTURE 2

Ben is a fifteen-year-old

_____ .

PICTURE 3

The name of this _____

is Tina.

PICTURE 4

It is eight o'clock in the

_____ .

B. Complete this exercise.

1. Name two rooms in a house.

   a. _____   b. _____

2. Name two people in a family.

   a. _____   b. _____

Comparing Old and New Concepts

1. Look at the people in Picture 1 on page 7. Is your family the same or different?

2. Look at the bedroom in Picture 2 on page 7. Is your bedroom the same or different?

3. Here is the schedule of a man named Henry Smith:

6:00 A.M.	awake	6:00 P.M.	in the car
7:00 A.M.	in the kitchen	7:00 P.M.	in the living room
9:00 A.M.	at work	10:00 P.M.	in the bedroom
12:30 P.M.	in a restaurant	11:30 P.M.	asleep in bed
3:00 P.M.	at work		

Here are some places people can be:

at a gas station	in the car	in a bus
in the house	on the lawn	at church
in a store	around the house	in a coffee shop
in the bedroom	with my children	on the street
at home	at school	

Now think of a typical day in your life and fill in the following schedule.

6:00 A.M.	_____
7:00 A.M.	_____
9:00 A.M.	_____
11:00 A.M.	_____
12:30 P.M.	_____
3:00 P.M.	_____
6:00 P.M.	_____
7:00 P.M.	_____
10:00 P.M.	_____
11:30 P.M.	_____
1:00 A.M.	_____

Look at your classmates' schedules. Is your schedule different from their schedules?

Getting Ready to Read

1. Developing New Concepts and Vocabulary

PART I

A. Say something about these pictures.   Use the new words.

PICTURE 1

PICTURE 2

father   family   typical   unusual

PICTURE 3

PICTURE 4

driver   policeman   park   yell (at)

B. Answer these questions.   Give your opinion.

1. Are these families typical or unusual?
2. Which scene is typical, Picture 3 or Picture 4?

PART II

A. Study Pictures 1, 2, 3, 4, and 5 and the new words and phrases.

PICTURE 1

open
ask
question
look

PICTURE 2

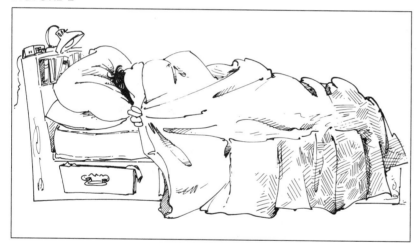

blanket
over
head

<u>phrase</u>
be in bed

PICTURE 3

tell

<u>phrase</u>
get up

14

PICTURE 4

phrase
make coffee

PICTURE 5

brother
sleep

phrase
pull off

B. Say something about Pictures 1, 2, 3, 4, and 5. Use the new words and phrases.

C. Is there anything unusual in these pictures? What do you think?

_____

_____

_____

_____

_____

2. Thinking and Questioning

A. Study these pictures and the new phrase.

PICTURE 1

phrase

be the boss

PICTURE 2

B. Say something about these two pictures. Use the new phrase.

C. Which sentence is true most of the time? Circle one.

1. Mothers usually get their children up.

2. Children usually get their mothers up.

D. Which sentence is true most of the time? Circle one.

1. Sarah Lewis usually gets her children up.

2. Sarah's children usually get her up.

E. Think about Picture 2. Do you have a question? Write it here:

_____ ?

Reading

Study these new words and phrases. Then read the story.

after	move	phrases	go to work	look at
dress	okay	Come on!	have school	be tired
eye	shoe	make a noise	Go away.	go back (to)
go (to/out)	some	be time to __	Stop it.	
good	want	have to	a lot (of)	

Hey, Who's the Mom Around Here?

Tina and Carol open the door to their mother's bedroom. They look in the room. Their mother is in bed—asleep.

Carol: Mom! It's after 7:30.

Sarah pulls the blanket over her head.

Tina: Mom, come on! Get up.

Sarah makes a noise, but she does not move.

Tina: Really, Mom, it's time to get up.
Carol: It's 7:30. You have to go to work and we have school.
Sarah: Go away.

Tina goes to the bed and pulls the blanket.

Sarah: Stop it. I want to sleep.

Carol goes to the door.

Tina: Where are you going?
Carol: To the kitchen. You get Mom up.
Tina: Okay. Make some coffee.
Carol: Okay.

Carol goes out the door.

Tina: Carol! Make a lot of coffee!
Carol: Okay.
Tina: Come on, Mom. Here's a dress. Shoes. Where are your shoes? Here they are. Come on. It's after 7:30. You have to go to work. Open your eyes, Mom.

Tina pulls off the blankets. Sarah opens her eyes and looks at Tina.

Tina: Come on, Mom.
Sarah: I'm tired. I want to go back to sleep.
Tina: No. You can't. Get up.
Sarah: Hey, who's the mom around here?
Tina: That's a good question.

Comprehension Activities

1. Reviewing the Story

Circle the correct answer.

1. Tina and Carol want their mother to

    a. make coffee.

    b. go to sleep.

    c. get up.

2. Sarah, their mother, wants to

    a. get up.

    b. go back to sleep.

    c. go to work.

3. Tina says that her mother has to

    a. go to work.

    b. go to school.

    c. go to the kitchen.

4. Tina asks her mother

    a. where the coffee is.

    b. where her shoes are.

    c. where she is going.

5. Sarah asks Tina

    a. who is making coffee in the kitchen.

    b. what time it is.

    c. who the mother is in their house.

MORE DIFFICULT QUESTIONS

Answer the following questions.

1. Why is Sarah asleep at 7:30?

2. Why does Sarah ask, "Hey, who's the mom around here?"

3. Is the Lewis family a typical family? Explain your answer.

2. Wondering About the Story

Think about the story. What do you want to know? Write a question here:

_____

_____ ?

3. Making a Guess

A. Read the last four lines of the story. If Sarah says something more to Tina, what will she say? Circle *a*, *b*, or *c*.

Sarah: I'm tired. I want to go back to sleep.
 Tina: No. You can't. Get up.
Sarah: Hey, who's the mom around here?
 Tina: That's a good question.

Sarah: a. Thank you, Tina. You're a good girl.

   b. Okay, okay. I'm getting up.

   c. Get out of here. I'm going back to sleep.

B. Discuss your answer with your classmates.

C. Read the following statements. What do you think about them? Check *True*, *False*, or *Need more information*.

1. Sarah is a mother.   ___ True ___ False ___ Need more information

2. Sarah is a good mother.   ___ True ___ False ___ Need more information

3. Sarah is a bad mother.   ___ True ___ False ___ Need more information

4. Sarah is a student.   ___ True ___ False ___ Need more information

5. Carol is a student.   ___ True ___ False ___ Need more information

6. Sarah works.   ___ True ___ False ___ Need more information

7. Tina works.   ___ True ___ False ___ Need more information

8. Tina is the boss in the
   Lewis family.   ___ True ___ False ___ Need more information

9. Tina is the boss in the
   Lewis family today.   ___ True ___ False ___ Need more information

Vocabulary Practice

A. Write about this picture. Use vocabulary from the story and the words and phrases next to the picture.

_____

_____

phrases

hold on (to)

birthday card

hold

present

birthday

behind

back

B. Complete these exercises. Use vocabulary from the story.

1. You want someone to get up. What can you say? Write three things.

   a. _____

   b. _____

   c. _____

2. Someone wants you to get up. You want to sleep. What can you say to that person? Write two things.

   a. _____

   b. _____

Comparing Old and New Concepts

1. Sarah's children have to wake her up in this story.
   How do you get up in the morning?
   Does a person get you up?
   Do you use a clock or a radio?

2. Today Sarah's children get up first.
   Who usually gets up first in the Lewis family?
   Who usually gets up first in your family?

Getting Ready to Read

1. Developing New Concepts and Vocabulary

A. Study Pictures 1, 2, and 3 and the new words and phrases.

PICTURE 1

phone
ring

<u>phrase</u>
pick up

PICTURE 2

accident
Honda
Chevrolet

<u>phrase</u>
be hurt

ambulance

talk

phrase

police officer

B. Say something about Pictures 1, 2, and 3. Use the new words and phrases.

2. Thinking and Questioning

A. Study this picture and the new words.

husband

cry

B. Say something about this picture with your classmates. Use the new words.

C. Think about the picture. Do you have any questions? Write two here.

1. _____ ?

2. _____ ?

Reading

Study these new words and phrases. Then read the story.

again	friend	late	**phrases**	I'm afraid (that)
alone	have	never	10:00 P.M.	be with ___
blue	hello	now	of course	
California	hospital	think (about)	be all right	
die	hour	week	⚠ Oh, (my) God.	
feel	know	wonder	be sorry	

The Quiet Hours

It is 1982. Sarah Lewis is at home. The children are asleep. It is 10:00 P.M. Ed Lewis, Sarah's husband, is not home. Sarah wonders, "Where is he? He's never this late. Maybe he's at work. No. It's too late for that. Maybe he's with Charlie. No. Charlie's in California this week. Maybe he's . . . If he's with another woman . . . No, not Ed."

The phone rings. Sarah looks at it. It rings again. She says, "It's Ed. I know it's Ed." She picks up the phone and says, "Hello." But it is not Ed.

Officer: Mrs. Lewis?
 Sarah: Yes. Who's this?
Officer: This is Officer Ames, Mrs. Lewis.
 Sarah: Officer?
Officer Yes, I'm with the Bristol Police.
 Sarah: My husband . . .
Officer: Mrs. Lewis?
 Sarah: Yes.
Officer: Is your husband's name Edward Lewis?
 Sarah: Yes. Why?
Officer: Do you have a blue, 1982 Chevrolet?
 Sarah: Oh, God. An accident.
Officer: Mrs. Lewis. Do you have . . .
 Sarah: Yes. Of course we do. A Chevrolet. What is it? Is Ed all right?
Officer: I'm sorry, Mrs. Lewis.
 Sarah: Oh, my God. Is he hurt?
Officer: I'm sorry. At 8:00 P.M. . . . .
 Sarah: Where is he? Is he in the hospital?
Officer: Mrs. Lewis, I'm afraid your husband died. Mrs. Lewis? Mrs.
        Lewis? Joe! Call the Madison police. Tell them to go to 106
        Greenwood. The Lewis house. Now! Mrs. Lewis? Are you there?

It is 1987 now. Sarah is not alone—she has her friends and her children—but she feels alone. Early in the morning when it is dark and quiet, Sarah thinks about Ed. Five years is a long time for some people, but not for Sarah.

Comprehension Activities

1. Reviewing the Story

Circle the correct answer.

1. At the beginning of the story, Sarah is

    a. at work.

    b. at home.

    c. in her car.

2. It is

    a. early in the morning.

    b. late at night.

3. The phone rings and it is

    a. Ed.

    b. Charlie.

    c. Officer Ames.

4. The policeman tells Sarah that Ed

    a. is in the hospital.

    b. died.

    c. is hurt.

5. Sarah feels alone because

    a. she doesn't have Ed.

    b. she doesn't have children.

    c. she doesn't have friends.

MORE DIFFICULT QUESTIONS

Answer the following questions.

1. Why is Sarah thinking about Ed at the beginning of the story?

    _____

2. Why is Sarah thinking about Ed at the end of the story?

    _____

2. Wondering About the Story

Think about the story. What do you want to know? Write a question here:

_____ ?

3. Making a Guess

A. Answer this question: Why do you think Sarah is still alone?

I think she is still alone because _____

B. Compare your answer with your classmates' answers.

A MORE DIFFICULT QUESTION

Imagine this situation: One day, when Sarah is at work, a man who works in her office invites her to go out for dinner.
What do you think Sarah says to the man? Write what she says here:

Sarah: _____

Discuss your answer with your classmates.

Vocabulary Practice

A. Look at the word and the picture:

house

Circle the words in the following list that you feel go with the word "house."

bedroom	window	green	police
lawn	week	door	white
eye	church	kitchen	school
street	restaurant	accident	blue

B. Now look at this word and the picture:

accident

Circle the words that you feel go with the word "accident."

week	police	house	white
officer	car	hospital	hello
say	nice	quiet	know
alone	die	hurt	happy

Comparing Old and New Concepts

1. Look at Picture 3 on page 22.
   Is this a typical automobile accident?
   Are people usually this quiet?
   Do people ever shout and yell?

2. Sarah stops talking after the policeman tells her about her husband's accident.
   Do most people react like Sarah?
   How else do people react when they hear very bad news?
   Do women react differently from men?

Getting Ready to Read

1. Developing New Concepts and Vocabulary

A. Study Pictures 1, 2, 3, 4, 5, and 6 and the new words and phrases.

PICTURE 1

refrigerator

hungry

PICTURE 2

study

write

composition

English

math

science

PICTURE 3

PICTURE 4

play
baseball
try
catch
ball
run
right
left

PICTURE 5

late

phrases
get to __
be in class

PICTURE 6

short

B. Say something about Pictures 1, 2, 3, 4, 5, and 6. Use the new words
and phrases.

2. Thinking and Questioning

A. Study this picture and the new word and phrases.

sad

phrases
be the matter (with)
make _____
   feel better
!screw up

B. Say something about the picture. Use the word and phrases next to the picture.

C. Think about the picture. Do you have any questions? Write two here:

1. _____ ?

2. _____ ?

Reading

Study these new words and phrases. Then read the story.

		phrases	
always	say		have a test
bad	!"Shrimp"	all the time	have a disease
brain	true	be wrong with __	be embarrassing
close	walk	do __ right	have a __ time
just	year	What do you mean?	a little
life			

30

I Screw Up All the Time.

Carol is in the kitchen when Ben walks in.

Carol: Hey, Ben.

Ben does not say anything.

Carol: What's wrong with you?
  Ben: Nothing.

Ben looks in the refrigerator.

Carol: Hungry?
  Ben: No.

Ben closes the refrigerator door.

Carol: You're not hungry? Something's wrong. You're always hungry.
  Ben: Nothing's wrong.
Carol: Okay. Nothing's wrong. So . . . tell me . . . how's school?

Ben does not answer.

Carol: That bad, huh? What's the problem—math?
  Ben: Math, English, science . . . you name it, I've got problems with it.
Carol: But you study, don't you?
  Ben: I can't do anything right.
Carol: What do you mean?
  Ben: I screw up.
Carol: Oh.
  Ben: I screw up all the time.
Carol: Mmmm.
  Ben: Like, I study math all night. Do we have a test in math? No, we
        have one in English. I get up early, but I get to school late. I
        screw up all the time.
Carol: Well, how's baseball?
  Ben: Don't ask. I screw up there, too. I go right, and the ball goes left.
        Something's wrong with me. Maybe I have a brain disease.
Carol: Ben!
  Ben: And I'm short. I'm the shortest guy in class. It's embarrassing.
Carol: Oh, Ben. You're not that short.
  Ben: I am too. They call me "Shrimp."
Carol: They don't.
  Ben: Yes, they do. It's true.
Carol: Oh, Ben. You're not so short. Maybe you screw up a little, but
        you're okay. You're just having a bad year.
  Ben: A bad year? I'm having a bad life.

Comprehension Activities

1. Reviewing the Story

A. Write the correct answers.

Ben says, "There's something wrong with me." Write two examples he gives.

1. _____

2. _____

B. Circle the correct answer.

1. In this story, Ben feels

    a. good.

    b. okay.

    c. bad.

2. After Carol talks with Ben, she thinks that

    a. Ben has problems, but is okay.

    b. Ben has something wrong with him.

    c. Ben has a brain disease.

2. Wondering About the Story

A. Think about the story. What do you want to know? Write a question here:

_____ ?

B. Answer these questions.

1. What do you think of Ben?

    _____

    _____

2. How serious are his problems?

    _____

    _____

3. Do you think Ben is a typical fifteen-year-old boy?

    _____

    _____

3. Making a Guess

A. Read the following statements. What do you think about them? Check *True*, *False*, or *Need more information*.

1. Ben is hungry. ___ True ___ False ___ Need more information
2. Ben is a good student. ___ True ___ False ___ Need more information
3. Ben is short. ___ True ___ False ___ Need more information
4. Ben is a good baseball player. ___ True ___ False ___ Need more information
5. Ben has many friends. ___ True ___ False ___ Need more information
6. There is something wrong with Ben. ___ True ___ False ___ Need more information
7. Ben has a brain disease. ___ True ___ False ___ Need more information
8. Ben has problems with math. ___ True ___ False ___ Need more information
9. Ben has problems with English. ___ True ___ False ___ Need more information
10. Ben screws up a lot. ___ True ___ False ___ Need more information

B. Answer these questions.

1. How do you think Ben feels after he talks to Carol?

_____

2. How do you think Carol feels about her brother?

_____

Vocabulary Practice

A. Look at this word:

school

Circle the words in the following list that you feel go with the word "school."

study	write	disease	class
walk	shrimp	English	phone
officer	church	refrigerator	coffee
test	math	science	morning
year	left	composition	sorry

B. Look at this word:

Ben

Circle the words that you feel go with the person named Ben in this book.

short	dummy	late	house
asleep	bad	sad	refrigerator
car	boy	quiet	tired
baseball	hungry	small	disease

Comparing Old and New Concepts

1. In the United States, baseball is a very popular sport.
   Do you like baseball?
   What other sports do you like?

2. In this story, Ben tells his problems to his sister, Carol.
   Do boys usually talk to their sisters about their problems?
   Do girls talk to their brothers?
   Who do you talk to?

MORE DIFFICULT QUESTIONS

In this story, Ben, who is fifteen years old, is worried about how tall he is and about his school work.
What other things do fifteen-year-olds worry about?
What do people your age worry about?

Getting Ready to Read

1. Developing New Concepts and Vocabulary

A. Study Pictures 1, 2, 3, and 4 and the new words and phrases.

PICTURE 1

need

flat

tire

bike

<u>phrases</u>

get ___ fixed

wait (for)

PICTURE 2

read

buy

PICTURE 3

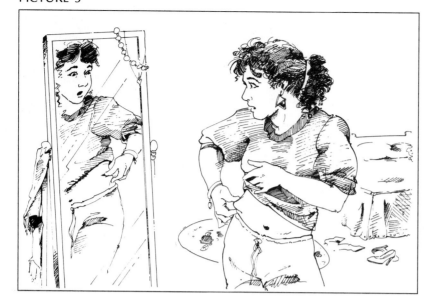

mirror

like

fat

phrase

the way ___ look

PICTURE 4

sit

desk

checkbook

money

bank

bill

B. Say something about Pictures 1, 2, 3, and 4. Use the new words and phrases.

2. Thinking and Questioning

A. Study this picture and the new words.

look

upset

hand

B. Say something about the picture. Use the new words.

C. Think about the picture. Do you have any questions? Write two here:

1. _____ ?

2. _____ ?

Reading

Study these new words and phrases. Then read the story.

believe	important	phrases	That's enough!
come	leave	have time for ___	You've got to be kidding!
down	please	All right.	Let me think about it.
first	really	Speak up.	care about ___
get	speak	What ___ for?	

You Never Have Time for Me.

Sarah is sitting at her desk. Her head is in her hands. Ben walks into the room.

Ben: Mom? I have to talk to you.
Sarah: Not now, Ben.
Ben: But I really need to talk to you. Please?
Sarah: Okay. What is it?
Ben: Um . . . well . . . I need . . .
Sarah: Don't tell me you need money. Please don't tell me you need money.
Ben: Well . . . I . . .
Sarah: All right. What is it?

Ben looks down and speaks quietly.

Ben: . . . $27.00.
Sarah: What? Speak up.

Ben looks up at his mother.

Ben: I need $27.00. It's important.
Sarah: Oh, no. I can't believe it.
Ben: Mom, I really need it.
Sarah: Well, what do you need it for?
Ben: Well, I need to get a tire fixed on my bike.
Sarah: And that costs $27.00?
Ben: No, $10.00. Mom, I have to have my bike.
Sarah: And what do you need the other $17.00 for?
Ben: (*Quietly*) A book on baseball.
Sarah: What?
Ben: A book on baseball. There's this book, and I really need it.
Sarah: You've got to be kidding!

Tina comes into the room.

Tina: Mom, can I talk to you?
Ben: *I'm* talking to her, dummy.
Tina: Well, I need to talk to Mom—alone.
Ben: Too bad. I'm first.
Tina: Mom!
Sarah: Ben . . .
Ben: She can wait!
Tina: *You* wait.
Ben: No!
Sarah: Stop it, you two.
Ben: That's right. (*To Tina*) You're upsetting Mom. So, leave!
Tina: *You* leave!
Sarah: All right. That's enough! Ben, about the book . . . I'm sorry. We don't have the money. And the tire . . . let me think about it, all right?
Ben: Mom!
Sarah: Now, let me talk to Tina.
Ben: You always have time for Tina. You never have time for me. She gets everything.
Sarah: Ben, that's not true.
Ben: Yes, it is.
Sarah: Ben!
Ben: You don't care about me! You never do!

Ben runs out of the room.

Sarah: Ben! Come here!

Sarah listens to Ben run downstairs. She sits quietly and looks down at her hands.

Sarah: Oh, Ben.

Note: Reading Punctuation and Italics

Read the following pairs of sentences out loud. Say each sentence differently.

1. Well, I need some money.

   Well . . . I need . . . some money.

2. I'm talking to her.

   I'm talking to her.

3. I need to talk to Mom alone.

   I need to talk to Mom—alone.

Comprehension Activities

1. Reviewing the Story

A. Circle the correct answer.

1. Ben wants to talk to his mother because

   a. he wants a new bike.

   b. he likes to talk to her.

   c. he needs some money.

2. At the end of the story,

   a. Ben agrees with his mother.

   b. Ben is upset and leaves the room.

   c. Sarah agrees with Ben.

3. Sarah does not want to talk about money because

   a. she does not have any money to give the children.

   b. her children ask her for money all the time.

   c. Tina and Ben are yelling at each other.

4. When his sister comes into the room, Ben gets

   a. quiet.

   b. upset.

   c. happy.

B. Answer the following questions.

1. How does Ben feel about his sister Tina?

   _____

   _____

2. How does his mother feel at the end of the story?

   _____

   _____

2. Wondering About the Story

Think about the story. What do you want to know? Write a question here:

_____

_____?

3. Making a Guess

Answer the following questions.

1. What do you think Tina wants to talk to her mother about?

   _____

2. Why do you think Ben and Tina have problems with each other?

   _____

3. How much money do you think Sarah is going to give Ben?

   _____

MORE DIFFICULT QUESTIONS

A. All of the answers below are possible. Choose the answer that you think is best. Circle *a*, *b*, or *c*.

1. If Sarah gives Ben $27.00,

   a. he will be happy.

   b. he will love Tina.

   c. he will get his tire fixed and buy the baseball book.

2. If Ben buys the baseball book,

   a. he will be a good player.

   b. he will still have problems playing baseball.

   c. he will not read it.

B. Discuss your answers with your classmates.

Vocabulary Practice

A. Look at this word:

problem

Circle the words that go with the word "problem."

leave	bike	baseball	bookstore
money	bill	fat	ugly
English	upset	letter	month

B. Look at the following words and phrases:

enough   don't let   money

speak up can't believe leave

Read the sentences below. Then choose one word or phrase from the list to complete each sentence.

1. When people have a lot of _____, they can buy anything they want.

2. I lock the door when I _____ the house.

3. I say "Please _____" when I can't hear what someone is saying on the telephone.

4. I _____ how much some cars cost today.

5. I guess I don't get _____ sleep. I'm always tired.

6. Parents usually _____ small children play in the street.

Comparing Old and New Concepts

1. Ben's bike is very important to him. He uses it to get around.
   How do you get around?
   Do you know many people who use bikes?

2. Ben and Tina fight with each other.
   Do you think it is unusual for brothers and sisters to fight?

3. The Lewises have money problems.
   Do you know anyone who has money problems?
   What kind of problems do they have?
   Is there anything they can do?

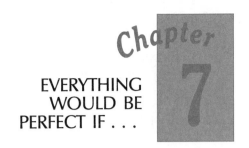
Getting Ready to Read

1. Developing New Concepts and Vocabulary

A. Study Pictures 1, 2, and 3 and the new words and phrases.

PICTURE 1

dentist

cavity

tooth/teeth

PICTURE 2

<u>phrase</u>

make an
appointment

join

cost

month

<u>phrase</u>
health club

B. Say something about Pictures 1, 2, and 3. Use the new words and phrases.

2. Thinking and Questioning

A. Study this picture and the new words and phrase.

hear

over

ear

<u>phrase</u>
be surprised

B. Say something about the picture. Use the new words and phrase.

C. Think about the picture. Do you have any questions? Write two here:

1. _____ ?

2. _____ ?

Reading

Study these new words and phrases.   Then read the story.

ago	listen	ugly	Oh, really?
beautiful	little	young	Get out (of here)!
enough	only		go out
ever	perfect	phrases	⚠ You're history!
Friday	put	Come on.	
hate	Saturday	spend time with ___	
⚠ jerk	see		

Everything Would Be Perfect If . . .

Tina and Sarah, her mother, are talking about Ben.

Tina: He's all right, Mom.
Sarah: Maybe he's right—I don't spend enough time with him.
Tina: Mom, I have to talk to you.
Sarah: Maybe . . .
Tina: Mom! I have to talk to you.
Sarah: All right. What is it?
Tina: Mom, I . . . uh . . .
Sarah: What's the matter, Tina?
Tina: Nothing. It's just . . . I hate myself.
Sarah: What? Why?

Tina hears a noise. She looks at the door.

Tina: Ben! Is that you? Go away!
Sarah: There's no one there. Come on. Tell me. What's wrong?
Tina: Mom, I'm so . . . fat.
Sarah: You're not fat, Tina.
Tina: And ugly.
Sarah: You're not ugly.
Tina: Fat and ugly. I am.
Sarah: No, you're not.

Ben looks into the room.

Ben: She's fat, Mom, and ugly, too.
Tina: Ben, get out of here!
Sarah: Ben. Get out. It's wrong to listen. Go downstairs.

Continued

Ben leaves. Tina goes to the door and yells at him.

Tina: Ben Lewis, I hate you!
Sarah: Tina! Don't say that. He's your brother. Come on. Sit down. Let's talk.

Tina sits on her mother's bed.

Tina: All my friends go out on Fridays and Saturdays. I never go out.
Sarah: You do. What about that boy, Henry, two weeks ago?
Tina: Oh, Mom, he's a jerk. Everyone knows he's a jerk.
Sarah: Oh, really?
Tina: The boys in school . . . they don't talk to me, they don't look at me. I walk by and they don't want to look at me. I'm fat—that's the problem. Everything would be perfect if I could join a health club.
Sarah: What?
Tina: I wouldn't be fat. You see? I'd be beautiful. Really, Mom. And it doesn't cost that much.
Sarah: Tina, I know you think you're fat. But really, you're not. You're only sixteen. And lots of girls when they're young are a little . . .
Tina: You see? You think I'm fat, too.
Sarah: Tina!
Tina: Mom, really. It's the answer. I know it is. If I joined a health club, then I'd be beautiful. Everything would be perfect. Don't you see?
Sarah: Tina . . .
Tina: Please, Mom. It's only $50.00 a month.
Sarah: $50.00! We don't have it.
Tina: Please, Mom. This is really important to me.

Ben comes into the room.

Ben: Mom! What about my tire?
Tina: You little jerk! Get out of here!

Carol comes into the room.

Carol: What's going on in here? Why all the noise?
Tina: I'm trying to talk to Mom.
Carol: Oh? Well, I need to talk to her, too.
Ben: Oh, yeah? What about? Are you fat, too?
Tina: You're history, Ben!
Carol: Mom. You know my appointment with the dentist? Well, I have to go again. I have four . . .
Sarah: Oh, no. No, no, no. I don't want to hear this.

Sarah puts her hands over her ears.

Sarah: Get out. Everyone! Get out! I don't want to hear any more.
Carol: Come on. Let's go.

The children leave the room. Sarah sits alone at her desk. She looks at the bills on her desk.

Sarah: What am I going to do? Ed, where are you when I need you? Everything would be perfect if you were here.

Comprehension Activities

1. Reviewing the Story

Circle the correct answer.

1. Tina wants to talk to her mother because

    a. she wants money to join a health club.

    b. she is fat.

    c. she has problems with boys.

2. Tina hates herself because

    a. she is fat and ugly.

    b. she thinks she is fat and ugly.

    c. all the boys are jerks.

3. Carol comes into the room to tell her mother that

    a. she has to make an appointment with the dentist.

    b. she is fat and ugly.

    c. she is going to need money for the dentist.

A MORE DIFFICULT QUESTION

Read the question in Column 1. Choose an answer from Column 2. Draw a line from the question to the correct answer.

Column 1	Column 2
What does Carol want?	Money for a tire and a book.
What does Ben want?	Money to join a health club.
What does Tina want?	Money for the dentist.
What does Sarah want?	Money to pay the bills.

2. Wondering About the Story

Think about the story. Do you have any questions? Write one here:

_____ ?

3. Making a Guess

Answer the following questions.

1. Does Tina feel better after she talks to her mother? Why or why not?

_____

_____

2. How does Sarah feel at the end of the story?

_____

_____

3. What will Sarah do about her money problems?

_____

_____

MORE DIFFICULT QUESTIONS

Circle the correct answer.

1. Which statement is true?

    a. Ben really thinks that Tina is fat and ugly.

    b. Ben says that Tina is fat and ugly just to upset her.

    c. Ben says that Tina is fat and ugly because he wants her to get money for the health club.

2. Which of Tina's problems came first?

    a. Tina got fat first. Then the boys stopped talking to her.

    b. The boys stopped talking to Tina. Then she got fat.

3. When Tina says, "You're history, Ben!" what does she mean?

    a. Ben likes history.

    b. Tina would like to kill Ben.

    c. Tina is going to kill Ben.

Vocabulary Practice

A. Look at the following words and phrases:

old	typical	a good student
ugly	quiet	a bad student
upset	short	a good mother
tired	unusual	a good brother
sad	fat	a bad mother
alone	hungry	a bad brother

Choose five words and phrases that describe Sarah. Write them below.

a. _____

b. _____

c. _____

d. _____

e. _____

Choose five words and phrases that describe Ben. Write them below.

a. _____

b. _____

c. _____

d. _____

e. _____

B. Look at the following words and phrase:

beautiful	put	spend time with
hate	perfect	

Read the sentences below. Then choose one word or phrase to complete each sentence.

1. My English is not _____ so I'm still going to school to study it.

2. I think Paris is a _____ city.

3. I like to _____ my friends.

4. I _____ my hands over my ears when people yell at me.

5. Some people _____ to get up in the morning.

Comparing Old And New Concepts

1. Tina wants to join a health club.
   Do you go to a health club?
   Would you like to join one?

2. Tina thinks it is important to be thin.
   Do you think it is important?
   Do you think "Thin is beautiful?"

3. When Sarah gets angry, she wants to be alone.
   Do you like to be alone when you are angry?
   Do you yell when you are angry?
   Is it better to hold your feelings inside or let them out?

4. Sarah and her children seem to fight a lot.
   Do you think most children talk to each other and to their parents the way they do in this story?

5. Some teenage problems are important. Some are not. Decide which problem below is most important. Write the number 1 after that phrase. Then choose the second most important problem. Write a 2 after it. Do this until each phrase has a number.

Teenage Problems	Importance
No money	_____
No boyfriend/girlfriend	_____
No car	_____
No one to talk to	_____
No friends	_____
No new clothes	_____
Problems with school	_____
Problems with alcohol/drugs	_____
Problems with health	_____
Problems with parents	_____
Bad skin	_____
Too fat	_____
Too thin	_____

   Your classmates may have very different answers. Discuss your answers with them.

Getting Ready to Read

1. Developing New Concepts and Vocabulary

A. Study these pictures and the new words and phrases.

PICTURE 1

secretary

office

smile

job

PICTURE 2

work

hard

<u>phrase</u>

get mad (at)

B. Say something about Pictures 1 and 2. Use the new words and phrase.

51

2. Thinking and Questioning

A. Study this picture.

B. Say something about the picture. What do you think is happening?

C. Do you have any questions about the picture? Write one here:

_____ ?

Reading

Study these new words and phrases. Then read the story.

Dad	phrases	give _____ trouble
last	Go ahead.	⚠ None of your business!
⚠ smartie	be to blame	get sick
	what else	

What's the Matter with Mom?

Carol, Tina, and Ben are talking in the kitchen.

Ben: What's the matter with Mom?
Tina: Yeah, something's really wrong. She never yells at us like that.
Carol: What did you say to her?
Ben: Nothing!
Carol: Well, you two are always fighting . . . .
Tina: Go ahead. Blame it on us. But you're the one who's always asking for money for the dentist.
Carol: So I'm to blame.
Ben: Something's wrong. Mom doesn't usually get that mad.
Carol: So, what do you think it is?
Ben: Dad.
Carol: Really?
Ben: Yeah. She's always saying "I wonder what your father would do?"
Tina: Yeah. And then she smiles and says, "I miss him."
Carol: I don't know. Maybe it's Dad, maybe it isn't.
Ben: Well, what else could it be?
Carol: Maybe it's her job. Her boss is giving her trouble again. The other secretary quit last week. And now Mom has to do her work and the work of the other secretary, too.
Ben: For the same money?
Carol: Uh-huh.
Tina: Slave driver! Mom should get another job.
Carol: She can't quit. We need the money.
Tina: So, do you think that's it? She's upset because of her job?
Ben: I don't think so.
Tina: So, smartie, what do you think it is?
Ben: Maybe it's her job. Who knows? Maybe it's my grades.
Tina: What's the matter with your grades?
Ben: None of your business!
Carol: Maybe she's just tired. She gets up so early to study. And she's working so hard.
Tina: Yeah, she does look tired.
Ben: What'll we do if Mom gets sick?
Tina: I don't know.
Ben: What would we do without Mom?

Comprehension Activities

1. Reviewing the Story

A. Answer the following questions.

1. How do the children know that something is really wrong with their mother?

2. At the end of the story, what are Tina and Ben most worried about?

B. Sarah is upset. The children give some reasons why they think she is upset. Write three of these reasons.

1.
2.
3.

C. Sarah is upset with her job. Write two reasons why she is upset with it.

1.
2.

2. Wondering About the Story

Do you have any questions about the story? Write one here:

_____?

3. Making a Guess

A. Check one sentence below.

What's the matter with Sarah?

____ Her children fight.

____ She's worried about money.

____ Her job is terrible.

____ Ben's grades are bad.

____ She is very tired.

____ She has too many things to do in her life.

B. Circle *1, 2, 3,* or *4.*

If Sarah is not happy with her job, I think she will:

1. find another job.

2. quit work and go to school.

3. sell her house and use that money to live.

4. look for a man with a lot of money.

MORE DIFFICULT QUESTIONS

Answer these questions.

1. If Sarah gets sick, what will the children do?

   _____

   _____

2. Do you think this book will have a happy ending?

   _____

   _____

   Why or why not?

   _____

   _____

3. How would you like this book to end?

   _____

   _____

Vocabulary Practice

A. Study this example:

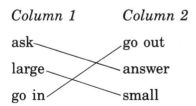

Column 1   *Column 2*

ask   go out

large   answer

go in   small

The words in Column 1 are the *opposite* of the words in Column 2. They are called *antonyms.*

Find a word in Column 1 that is the *antonym* of each word in Column 2. Draw a line from one word to the other.

Column 1	Column 2
beautiful	early
Dad	the same
different	leave
late	old
new	right
come in	listen
speak	ugly
left	Mom

B. Study this example:

Column 1   Column 2

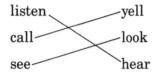

listen — yell
call — look
see — hear

The words in Column 1 have *the same* meaning as or a *similar* meaning to the words in Column 2. They are called *synonyms*.

Find a word in Column 2 that is a *synonym* for a word in Column 1. Draw a line from one word to the other.

Column 1	Column 2
mad	leave
quit	job
work	upset

C. Look at the following words and phrases:

blames ___ on ___   job   quit   fighting

gets mad at   smiles   without

Read the sentences below. Then choose one word or phrase to complete each sentence.

1. Ben says, "I don't like you." Tina says, "Well, I hate you, Ben Lewis."

   Ben and Tina are _____ again.

2. Sarah says, "I don't understand my boss. He says that I'm slow and I don't work hard enough."

   Sarah's boss _____ everything _____ her.

3. Sometimes, when Sarah drives her car, she yells out her window at the other drivers, "You jerk!"

   Sarah _____ the other drivers.

4. Sarah doesn't like her boss very much, and she feels she has too much work to do.

   Sarah would like to find a better _____.

5. Ben is not a very good student. He says, "When I'm 16, I'm not going to go to school anymore."

   Ben wants to _____ school when he is 16.

6. Carol sees Bill Albers in school every day. She likes him a lot.

   When Bill says, "Hi" to Carol, she _____.

7. Carol likes school more these days because she sees Bill Albers there each morning.

   Carol wouldn't like school as much _____ Bill.

Comparing Old and New Concepts

1. Some people like to work hard. They like to be busy, and they like to do something different every day. Other people want an easy job. They like to do the same thing every day. They do not want to work too hard. They believe that there are things in life that are more important than work.
   How do people you know feel about work?
   How do you feel?
   Do you want to be the boss someday?
   What do you think is more important than work?

2. Sarah sometimes gets mad at her children and at her boss.
   Do you ever get mad?
   If you do, who do you get mad at most?
   What makes you mad?

Chapter
9

Getting Ready to Read

1. Developing New Concepts and Vocabulary

A. Study Pictures 1, 2, 3, 4, 5, and 6 and the new words and phrases.

PICTURE 1

earn

deliver

paperboy

<u>phrases</u>

paper route

PICTURE 2

McDonald's

afternoon

PICTURE 3

sell

<u>phrase</u>
lemonade stand

PICTURE 4

record
spend
pay (for)
counter

PICTURE 5

<u>phrase</u>
football team

PICTURE 6

find

new

interview

phrase

get a job

B. Say something about Pictures 1, 2, 3, 4, 5, and 6. Use the new words and phrases.

2. Thinking and Questioning

A. Study this picture.

B. Say something about the picture. What do you think is happening?

C. Do you have any questions about the picture? Write one here:

_____ ?

Reading

Study these new words and phrases. Then read the story.

awful	stay	phrases	be embarrassing
college	stop	in a way	find out ___
guy	stupid	get by	have a choice
Miss	understand	help out	get/be serious
November		⚠ have (got) a	be amazing
		screw loose	⚠ Get off my case!

We Really Have a Problem.

Carol walks back into the kitchen. Ben and Tina are sitting there.

Tina: Well?
Ben: Did you talk to Mom?
Carol: Yes.
Tina: And?
Carol: We really have a problem.
Ben: *We* do?
Tina: What is it?
Carol: And Mom doesn't know what to do. She's so tired. And all she can
     do is talk about Dad.
Tina: Is that the problem?
Carol: What?
Tina: Dad. Is she thinking about Dad?
Carol: In a way. But the problem is money.
Tina: Money is always the problem around here. But we always get by.
Carol: Well, it's serious this time, Tina. Mom's job just doesn't pay enough.
     We have to do something. If we don't . . .
Tina: *We?*
Carol: That's right. All of us are going to have to help out.
Tina: What do you mean?
Carol: We'll have to stop spending money.
Tina: Stop? I don't have enough now.
Carol: Tina! You don't understand how serious this is.

Ben: She's got a screw loose.

Carol: We can't ask Mom for *any* money.

Tina: Okay, okay. So I won't join the health club. I'll just die all alone—fat and ugly.

Carol: The health club is just the beginning, Tina. We have to get jobs.

Tina: Jobs? No!

Ben: What's the matter with getting a job?

Tina: It's embarrassing.

Carol: We may not have a choice.

Tina: I'll die. I'll absolutely die. What if my friends find out that I have to work? I can't. I won't. It's just too awful.

Ben: Well, you two can get jobs. But I'm too young.

Tina: Oh, no you don't, Ben Lewis! No way! If I have to work, you have to work.

Ben: What can I do? You have to be sixteen to work.

Tina: Well . . . you can . . .

Ben: Yeah? Let's hear it.

Tina: . . . you can open a lemonade stand!

Ben: In November? Get serious.

Tina: Well, then, you can be . . . a paperboy!

Ben: A paperboy? Yeah. Well . . . Maybe. A paper route wouldn't be so bad.

Tina: It wouldn't?

Ben: No. Two or three guys I know have paper routes.

Tina: Oh.

Ben: So, Miss Perfect, what are you going to do?

Tina: Hey, listen. Maybe if I sell my records, I can join the health club.

Carol: Tina! Are you stupid or something?

Tina: What did I say?

Carol: You've got to stop thinking about yourself. We have to work to get money for *Mom*—not for us. She's talking about selling the house or maybe getting two jobs.

Tina: We can't sell the house. I'll die. What'll I tell my friends?

Carol: If Mom gets a second job, she'll have to quit college.

Tina: She can't quit. She'll never get a better job if she quits school.

Ben: Right. Finally your brain is working.

Tina: Ben! Get off my case!

Carol: Come on, you guys. Don't you see? If we work, maybe she can stay in school.

Tina: Well . . . uh . . . maybe I could get a job at McDonald's in the afternoons. It might not be so bad. Mary says all the guys on the football team go there after school.

Carol: Tina, you're amazing.

Tina: Why? What did I say?

Comprehension Activities

1. Reviewing the Story

A. Answer the following questions.

1. Why is Sarah Lewis so upset? What's the real problem?

_____

_____

2. Why does Tina get upset in this story?

_____

_____

3. Why doesn't Ben want to open a lemonade stand?

_____

_____

B. Circle the correct answer.

1. How does Carol feel about their problem?

   a. She does not want to do anything.

   b. She feels that the three kids will have to help their mother in some way.

   c. She feels that the three kids will have to quit school and go to work.

2. How does Tina feel about their problem?

   a. She feels that everything will be okay if Ben gets a job.

   b. She does not want to get a job, but she thinks she she may have to get one.

   c. She wants to quit school and go to work.

3. How does Ben feel about their problem?

   a. He thinks everything will be okay.

   b. He wants to get a job.

   c. He is not very happy about working.

2. Wondering About the Story

Do you have any questions about the story? Write one here:

_____

_____ _____ ?

3. Making a Guess

A. How do you think the Lewis children will help their mother?

1. Ben will _____

2. Carol will _____

3. Tina will _____

B. What do you think Sarah Lewis will do?

Sarah will _____

A MORE DIFFICULT QUESTION

Do you think the Lewis family will get out of trouble? Explain your answer.

_____

_____

_____

Vocabulary Practice

Look at the following words and phrases:

awful	sell	have a choice
understand	earn	have a screw loose
stay	paperboy	

Read the sentences below. Then choose one word or phrase to complete each sentence.

1. My brother wants to work as a _____ .

2. When I do not _____ what people say, I ask them to say it again.

3. When kids want to _____ money, they get part-time jobs.

4. In the United States, you do not _____; you have to go to school until you are sixteen years old.

5. I like to go to stores that _____ records and just look around.

6. Some women _____ at home when they have small children.

7. I think it is _____ for children to smoke cigarettes.

8. I do not like it when people tell me, "You _____."

Comparing Old and New Concepts

1. Many young people get jobs after school. Some of them take care of small children (babysit), take care of lawns, deliver papers, or do housework.
   Do you know any young people who work?
   If so, what do they do?

2. The Lewis children are thinking about getting jobs.
   Is it easy or difficult for young people to find work?
   Would it be easy or difficult for you to find a job today?

3. Many people like "fast-food" restaurants. They go to them for lunch.
   Sometimes the whole family goes to them for dinner.
   Name some fast-food restaurants. What do they sell?
   Do you like fast-food restaurants?
   When do you go to a fast-food restaurant?
   What kind of fast food do you like best?

WHAT IF
THEY DON'T
WANT ME?

Getting Ready to Read

1. Developing New Concepts and Vocabulary

A. Study Pictures 1, 2, and 3 and the new words and phrases.

PICTURE 1

comb	phrase
hair	look ___ best
floor	

PICTURE 2

phrases

part-time job

full-time job

	BEGIN WORK	END WORK	DAYS
SARAH	9:00 AM	5:00 PM	M-F
BEN	5:30 AM	7:00 AM	M-F
CAROL	9:00 AM	4:00 PM	SA-SU

PICTURE 3

stand

sign

phrases

in front (of)

help wanted

B. Say something about Pictures 1, 2, and 3. Use the new words and phrases.

2. Thinking and Questioning

A. Study these pictures and the new words and phrases.

PICTURE 1

order
wash

phrases
fall (madly) in love

PICTURE 2

cake

phrase
stuff ___self (with)

B. Say something about Pictures 1 and 2. Use the new words and phrases.

C. Do you have any questions about the pictures? Write one here:

_____ ?

Reading

Study these new words and phrases.   Then read the story.

care	mean	phrases	Who knows?
forever	relax	be willing	the ___ of ___
help		You're impossible.	dreams
inside		That's all there is to it.	take a look (at)
			be ready

What If They Don't Want Me?

Carol and Tina are standing in front of the McDonald's restaurant in Madison.   Carol already has a job at Tony's Restaurant.   Today she is trying to help Tina find a job.   McDonald's has a sign in the window: "Part-Time Help Wanted."

Carol: Let's go in.

Tina: Now?

Carol: Of course, now.   How long do you want to wait?

Tina: Forever!   Mom won't like it.

Carol: Come on, Tina.   Mom needs our help.

Tina: What if they don't want me?

Carol: Then we'll try somewhere else.   Come on.

Tina: Wait.   What do I say?   I can't think of anything to say.

Carol: Relax, will you?

Tina: What if they ask what kind of work I want to do?

Carol: Tell them you're willing to do anything.

Tina: Anything?   What if they ask me to wash floors?

Carol: Tell them you'll do it.

Tina: I will not.   What if my friends see me washing floors?

Carol: Who cares?

Tina: I care!

Carol: You're impossible.   Go home and stuff yourself with cake.

Tina: You're mean!   I'm going home.

Carol: Oh, no you're not.   Listen, Tina.   Mom needs money and we have to help her.   I have a job.   Now you're getting a job.   And that's all there is to it.   Now comb your hair, and let's go inside.   Who knows? Maybe the man of your dreams will walk in, order a hamburger, take one look at you, and fall madly in love.

Tina: Oh . . . I never thought of that.   Where's my comb?   I have to look my best.

Carol: Tina!

Tina combs her hair.

Tina: Okay.   I'm ready.

Carol: You're amazing.

Tina: I know.   Let's go.

Comprehension Activities

1. Reviewing the Story

Read the following statements. If the statement is true, write "T." If it is false, write "F."

1. _____ At the beginning of the story, Tina wants to work at McDonald's.

2. _____ At the beginning of the story, Carol wants Tina to work at McDonald's.

3. _____ Carol has a job at McDonald's.

4. _____ Tina thinks her mother will be happy if she gets a job.

5. _____ Tina does not want to wash floors.

6. _____ Tina does not care what her friends think.

7. _____ At the end of the story, Tina wants to work at McDonald's.

MORE DIFFICULT QUESTIONS

1. _____ In this story, Carol helps Tina a lot.

2. _____ Tina has experience in finding a job.

3. _____ Carol has experience in finding a job.

4. _____ Carol loses her patience with Tina.

5. _____ Tina does not want to fall in love.

6. _____ Tina thinks it is possible that she will find the man of her dreams at McDonald's.

7. _____ Carol thinks Tina is amazing because she combs her hair.

2. Wondering About the Story

Do you have any questions about the story? Write one here:

_____ ?

3. Making a Guess

Finish the following sentences.

1. Tina will go into McDonald's and she _____

_____

2. Later that night, Carol will tell her mother _____

_____

3. Their mother will _____

_____

Vocabulary Practice

A. Look at this word:

job

Circle the words that you feel go with the word "job."

ambulance	cake	money	quit	store
boy	English	part-time	relax	talk
bank	help wanted	quiet	restaurant	work

B. Look at these expressions:

You're impossible.   You've got a screw loose!

Get off my case!   That's all there is to it.

Who knows?

Choose the correct expression to complete each item below.

1. You're always telling me what to do. I'm forty-five years old.

   _____

2. Don't worry about your interview. You go in. You answer a few questions.
   You smile. You ask a few questions. _____

3. Go ahead. Ask your boss for more money. _____
   Maybe he'll give you more.

4. I talk and talk, but you don't listen. _____

5. You're going to ride your bike from New York to Los Angeles?

   _____

Comparing Old and New Concepts

1. When some employers have a job opening, they put a sign in their store
   window. The sign says "Help Wanted." Other employers put advertisements in
   the newspapers.
   What's the best way to find a job?
   How do people you know find jobs?

2. Tina wants to find a job. She is trying to look her best. Look at Picture 6 on
   page 61.
   Do you think she is wearing the right clothes?
   What do people you know wear when they are trying to find a job?

Chapter

11

Getting Ready to Read

1. Developing New Concepts and Vocabulary

A. Study these pictures and the new words.

PICTURE 1

dinner

BREAD

MILK

SALAD

SPAGHETTI
WITH SAUCE

PICTURE 2

cook

stove

table

B. Say something about Pictures 1 and 2. Use the new words.

2. Thinking and Questioning

A. Study these pictures and the new words and phrase.

PICTURE 1

kid
happy

<u>phrase</u>
smile (about)

PICTURE 2

kiss

B. Say something about the pictures. Use the new words and phrase.

C. Do you have any questions about the pictures? Write one question about each picture here:

1. _____ ?

2. _____ ?

Reading

Study these new words and phrases.   Then read the story.

awesome	kick	phrases	the rest (of)
give	Tuesday	go on	be settled
great	under	Wait a minute.	
hit	weekend	deliver papers	

Smiling

Sarah is sitting in the kitchen.   Dinner is cooking on the stove.   She wonders, "Where are the kids?   Let's see ... what day is today?   Tuesday.   It's Tuesday.   Ben has baseball today.   Uh-huh.   That's right.   I guess that's why he's late.   But what about Carol and Tina?"   The kitchen door opens, and Carol and Tina walk in, smiling.

Tina: Hi, Mom!
Carol: Hi, Mom!
Sarah: Well, you two look happy.   What are you smiling about?
Tina: Well ...
Carol: Let's wait for Ben.
Tina: I want to tell her now.
Sarah: Tell me what?

The kitchen door opens, and Ben walks in, smiling.

Ben: Hi!
Sarah: Another one smiling.   What's going on?
Ben: I got a hit today.
Sarah: That's great!
Ben: Yeah, it was awesome.
Sarah: I'm sure it was.   Well, dinner's ready.

They sit down at the kitchen table.

Ben: Spaghetti again?
Tina: Spaghetti forever.
Carol: So ... what do you think?   Should we tell Mom?
Sarah: Tell me what?
Tina: *I* have a job!
Sarah: No!
Tina: Yes!
Sarah: Where?
Tina: McDonald's.
Carol: And I have one at Tony's.   We think that you should stay in school, Mom.
Sarah: Oh, you do, do you?

Continued

Ben: I have a job, too. I have my own paper route.
Sarah: Wait a minute kids . . .
 Tina: You see? Mom doesn't like it.
Sarah: . . . what about school? When are you going to do your homework?
 Ben: I deliver papers before school.
Carol: And I work on weekends.
 Tina: And I work from 3:30 to 7:00.
Carol: We're going to keep $10.00 and give the rest of our money to you.
 Tina: We are?

Carol kicks Tina under the table.

 Tina: I mean . . . That's right. We are.
Carol: It's all settled, Mom.
Sarah: It is, is it?

Sarah looks at them silently. Then she smiles.

Sarah: Come here. I want to kiss you all.

Comprehension Activities

1. Reviewing the Story

Answer the following questions.

1. Why are Carol and Tina late for dinner?

2. Why isn't Ben home at the beginning of the story?

3. What are Carol and Tina smiling about when they come in the door?

4. Why is Ben happy when he comes in?

5. What are the kids going to do with the money from their jobs?

MORE DIFFICULT QUESTIONS

1. How happy is Sarah to hear that the children have jobs?

2. Why does Carol kick Tina under the table?

2. Wondering About the Story

Do you have any questions about the story? Write one here:

_____?

3. Making a Guess

Answer the following questions.

1. Which one of the children (Ben, Tina, Carol) has the best job?

_____

2. Which one of the children do you think will make the most money?

_____

3. Do you think Sarah will let the children keep their jobs?

_____

Vocabulary Practice

Look at the following words and phrases:

happy	Wait a minute.	give	the rest of	kisses
under	going on	awesome	weekend	is settled

Read the sentences below. Then choose one word or phrase to complete each sentence.

1. I love Julian Lennon, and I think his new record is _____.

2. In some countries, when a man meets a woman, he _____ her hand.

3. Sometimes when I eat, I take off my shoes _____ the table.

4. Why are you smiling? I don't understand. What's _____?

5. I can't wait. I'm going to a great concert this _____.

6. Okay. It _____. I'll meet you at 5:30 on Tuesday.

7. _____. I don't understand. Say that again.

8. I can't eat any more. You have _____ the pizza.

9. Gee, I'm hungry. _____ me two large hamburgers.

10. How are you? Are you _____? Is everything okay?

Comparing Old and New Concepts

1. Look at Picture 1 on page 73. Many Americans eat dinners like this one. What do people you know eat in the evening?

2. When Carol does not want Tina to talk, she kicks her under the table. What other things can you do to make someone be quiet?

3. The Lewises have to save money. Sarah tells the children that they cannot buy new clothes or records. The children got part-time jobs to help out. What else can the family do to get more money?

4. What do you do when you do not have enough money?

Getting Ready to Read

1. Developing New Concepts and Vocabulary

A. Study Pictures 1, 2, 3, 4, 5, and 6 and the new words and phrases.

PICTURE 1

supermarket

push

cart

aisle

fruit

phrase

spaghetti sauce

PICTURE 2

boyfriend
girlfriend

phrase

high school

PICTURE 3

Sarah and Ed
Wedding Day

marry

phrase
be in love (with)

PICTURE 4

APES

CHIMPANZEE ORANGUTAN   MONKEY   GORILLA

strong

big

PICTURE 5

monster

PICTURE 6

gun

rob

warn

kill

B. Say something about Pictures 1, 2, 3, 4, 5, and 6. Use the new words and phrases.

2. Thinking and Questioning

A. Study these pictures and the new words and phrase.

PICTURE 1

handsome

nice

PICTURE 2

<u>phrase</u>

be crazy about ___

PICTURE 3

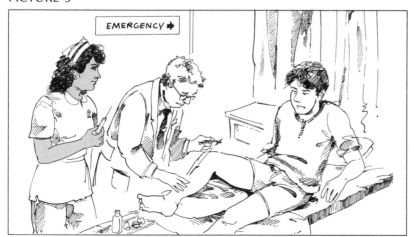

stitch

shot

B. Say something about the pictures. What do you think is happening?

C. Do you have any questions about the pictures? Write two here:

1. _____ ?

2. _____ ?

Reading

Study these new words and phrases. Then read the story.

absolutely	lie	phrases	be a dream
bum	live	be married (to)	Come to think of it . . .
call	peace	be divorced (from)	
continue	widow	get together	
cute	yet	say goodbye	

Love Is in the Air.

Sarah and Carol are buying food in the supermarket near their house.
They are walking up and down the aisles.

Sarah: What else do we need? Do we have enough fruit?
Carol: I think so.
Sarah: Okay. What else?
Carol: Spaghetti. We need more spaghetti . . . and sauce.
Sarah: Right.

They turn to the spaghetti aisle. Sarah looks up and stops. Carol
continues walking; then she stops and looks back at her mother. Sarah is
standing with her mouth open. She is looking at a man.

Sarah: Frank! Is that you?
Frank: Sarah?
Sarah: Frank!
Frank: You look great!
Sarah: So do you.
Frank: I can't believe it . . . after all these years.
Sarah: Twenty years.
Frank: And you're still living here in Madison?
Sarah: Yes. And what about you?
Frank: I'm living in Brighton, but I'm moving back to Madison next month.
Sarah: You are!

Continued

Frank turns to Carol. He smiles at her.

Frank: And who's this?
Sarah: This is Carol, my oldest daughter.
Frank: You have a daughter!
Sarah: Two daughters and a son.
Frank: Is that right! Well, hello, Carol. You're beautiful, like your mother.
Carol: Hello.
Sarah: Frank and I are old friends.

Frank and Sarah look at each other.

Frank: So, you're married?
Sarah: No. I'm a widow. And you, Frank?
Frank: I'm divorced.
Sarah: You're not married?
Frank: Um . . . listen . . . ah . . .
Sarah: Yes?
Frank: I'd like to call you when I get to town. Maybe we could get
       together and talk about old times.
Sarah: Yes. That would be nice, Frank.

Sarah and Frank say goodbye, and he walks away.

Carol: Mom! He's gorgeous!
Sarah: Is he?
Carol: "Is he?" Open your eyes, Mom. He's a dream!

    Later that evening, Tina comes into the kitchen. Ben and Carol are
talking.

 Ben: So, he's really a nice guy?
Carol: Absolutely. He's great.
 Tina: Who's great?
 Ben: Mom's new boyfriend.
 Tina: Mom has a boyfriend? Who?
Carol: Well, he's really an old boyfriend of hers from high school. His
       name is Frank, and he's so-o-o gorgeous.
 Tina: Well, I have a boyfriend, too.
 Ben: Another one?
 Tina: This time it's real.
 Ben: She's in love again.
 Tina: Carol, you were right. You said I would meet my dream man at
       McDonald's.
Carol: So, who's this dream man of yours?
 Tina: Peter Mannis.
 Ben: Peter Mannis! Oh, no!

Tina: He's so cute.
Ben: He's an ape.
Tina: He's so strong . . .
Ben: He's a gorilla!
Tina: . . . and big . . .
Ben: Frankenstein. This guy's a monster, believe me.
Carol: Ben.
Tina: He's a dream.
Ben: The guy has long hair on his hands.
Tina: He does not.

Sarah comes into the kitchen.

Sarah: Hi, kids. What's going on here?
Ben: Tina's in love with a bum.
Tina: Mom!
Ben: She's crazy about a guy who's always in trouble. This guy robs
banks.
Tina: That's a lie!
Carol: Come on, Ben. I think I know him. I don't think he robs
banks . . . yet.
Sarah: Tina! Who *is* this?
Tina: No one in this family understands me.
Ben: You're right about that. Hey, listen Mom. I've got to tell you
something. You're going to get a bill. Don't worry about it. I'll
pay it.
Sarah: What bill?
Ben: It's nothing—a hospital bill.
Sarah: What?
Ben: Yeah. You see, there's this big dog that waits for me on my paper
route—he's a monster. . . . You know? Come to think of it, this dog
looks a lot like Peter Mannis.
Tina: Ben, I'm warning you!
Sarah: What about the hospital, Ben?
Ben: Nothing to worry about, Mom—just a few stitches and a shot.
Sarah: I can't believe it. Just when I think everything is going to be
okay . . .
Carol: Don't worry, Mom. Everything will be perfect if you and Frank . . .
Tina: Yes, and if I marry . . .
Ben: And maybe I can get a gun and kill . . .
Sarah: Oh, my God!
Ben: What's the matter?
Sarah: Give me peace.
Carol: Peace? What's that?

Comprehension Activities

1. Reviewing the Story

A. Answer these questions.

1. Who do Sarah and Carol meet at the supermarket?

   _____

   _____

2. How does Ben feel about Peter Mannis?

   _____

   _____

B. Circle the correct answer.

1. How does Carol feel about Frank?

   a. She seems to be very worried.

   b. She is happy.

   c. She does not like him.

2. Frank says to Sarah, "Maybe we could get together and talk over old times." What do you think he means?

   a. He really just wants to talk to an old friend.

   b. He wants to see her because he likes her.

   c. He is just being polite.

3. Sarah answers, "That would be nice." What do you think she means?

   a. She wants to see Frank again.

   b. She really does not want to see him again.

   c. She is in love with Frank.

4. Ben says that Peter Mannis robs banks. What do you think he means?

   a. He really robs banks.

   b. He does not like the kind of person Peter is.

   c. He really likes Peter, and he is just joking.

5. Is Sarah worried at the end of the story?

   a. She is not worried.

   b. She is very worried.

   c. She is a little worried.

Answer these questions.

1. Why does Ben say that Peter has long hair on his hands?

   _____

2. Why does Sarah say, "Give me peace?"

   _____

2. Wondering About the Story

Do you have any questions about the story? Write one here:

_____?

3. Making a Guess

Answer this question:

If Frank comes to the Lewis house, how will the children feel about his visit?

_____

Vocabulary Practice

A. Look at these words.

old	bum	ape	unusual	alone
ugly	nice	big	sad	typical
tired	handsome	hurt	awesome	young
cute	crazy	happy	quiet	okay
strong	monster	mean	beautiful	

B. Now describe each person below.

1. Choose three words that describe Sarah. Write them here:

   a. _____

   b. _____

   c. _____

2. Choose three words that describe Ben. Write them here:

   a. _____

   b. _____

   c. _____

3. Choose three words that describe Carol. Write them here:

a. _____

b. _____

c. _____

4. Choose three words that describe Tina. Write them here:

a. _____

b. _____

c. _____

5. Choose three words that describe Frank. Write them here:

a. _____

b. _____

c. _____

6. Choose three words that describe Peter. Write them here:

a. _____

b. _____

c. _____

Comparing Old and New Concepts

1. Most Americans buy their food in large supermarkets. In some parts of the United States, people can buy food directly from farmers.
   Where do you buy your food?
   Do you go to different places or just to one store?

2. Many American teenagers have a boyfriend or a girlfriend when they get to high school.
   Do you think this is good, or do you think teenagers should wait until they are older?
   How old are kids you know when they begin to have a boyfriend or a girlfriend?

3. Kids love to read about monsters. They like to go to monster movies, too.
   Describe some monsters you know about.
   What countries are the stories about these monsters from?
   Do you like to hear or read about them?

Grammatical Structures[*]

Chapter 1

Pronouns
  it
  no one
  their

Nouns
  count
    singular
    plural

Articles
  the
  a

Conjunctions
  and
  but

Adverbs
  very
  no
  not
  there (subj.)

Verbs
  be
    is
    are

Prepositions
  in + place
  on + place

Chapter 2

Pronouns
  she
  her

Nouns
  possessive: *'s*
  possessive: *of*

Interrogative Words
  where
  what

Verbs
  simple present tense

Prepositions
  in + time

Clauses
  when + simple present

Chapter 3

Pronouns
  they
  you
  we
  I
  that
  your

Nouns
  mass

Verbs
  imperative
  present continuous
  modals
    have to
    can (prohibition)

  be
    am

* **To the teacher:** We have included this list of grammatical structures for your information. Recent research suggests that unknown grammatical structures often do not prevent readers from developing an accurate interpretation of the text. Therefore, while it may be helpful for students to learn the structures in advance of reading the text, it is not necessary that they be pretaught.

Chapter 4

Pronouns
them
this
my
he

Articles
an

Adjectives
this

Clauses
if + simple present

Interrogative Words
who

Adverbs
too

Prepositions
at + place
at + time

Phrases
too ___
infinitive

Chapter 5

Pronouns
anything
nothing
something
me

Interrogative Words
how

Conjunctions
so

Adjectives
superlative

Intensifiers
that
so

Chapter 6

Verbs
let + base form
imperative
negative
modals
can (possibility)

Adverbs
-ly adverbs

Adjectives
the other

Chapter 7

Pronouns
him
myself
everyone

Adverbs
just
all
ago
much
lots of
only
any
more

Verbs
Let's + base form
future
going to

Prepositions
on + time

Clauses
if + past
could
would

Chapter 8

Pronouns
  us
  one
  none

Interrogative Words
  what else

Adjectives
  another

Verbs
  past
  future
    will
  modals
    should

Conjunctions
  then

Phrases
  description
    like
  purpose
    for
  reason
    because of

Clauses
  description
    who

Chapter 9

Pronouns
  yourself

Verbs
  modals
    may
    might

Chapter 10

Pronouns
  our

Verbs
  help + base form

Interrogative Words
  how long

Adverbs
  already
  somewhere

Chapter 11

Prepositions
  on + time
  from + time *to* + time
  before

Chapter 12

Pronouns
  nothing

Verbs
  modals
    would like

Adverbs
  so

Prepositions
  near
  up
  down
  after
  back

Word List*

absolutely	12	Chevrolet	4
accident	4	children	2
after	3	church	1
again	4	close	5
ago	7	clothes	2
aisle	12	college	9
alone	4	comb	10
always	5	come	6
ambulance	4	composition	5
answer	2	continue	12
ape	12	cook	11
ask	3	cool	1
asleep	1	cost (v)	7
awake	1	cry	4
awesome	11	cute	12
awful	9		
		Dad	8
back	12	dark	1
bad	5	daughter	2
ball	5	dentist	7
bank	6	desk	6
baseball	5	die	4
beautiful	7	different	1
bed	2	dinner	11
bedroom	2	door	2
before	8	down	6
believe	6	dress	3
big	12	driver	3
bike	6	dummy	2
bill	6		
blanket	3	ear	7
blue	4	early	2
book	2	empty	1
boy	2	English	5
boyfriend	12	enough	7
brain	5	ever	7
brother	3	eye	3
building	1		
bum	12	family	3
buy	6	fat	6
		father	3
cake	10	feel	4
California	4	find	9
call	3	first	6
call (telephone)	12	flat	6
car	1	floor	10
catch	5	food	9
cavity	7	forever	10
checkbook	6	Friday	7

* Numbers indicate chapters where words first appear in the book.

92

friend	4	listen	7
fruit	12	little	7
		live	12
get	6	long	4
girl	2	look	6
give	11		
go (to/out)	3	make	3
good	3	man	1
gorgeous	12	map	1
great	11	marry	12
green	1	math	5
gun	12	maybe	2
guy	9	McDonald's	9
		mean (*adj*)	10
hair	12	mention	8
hamburger	10	mirror	6
hand	6	Miss	9
happy	11	Mom	2
hard	8	money	6
hate	7	month	7
head	3	morning	2
hear	7	mother	2
hello	4	mouth	12
help	10	move	3
hit (*n*)	11		
Honda	4	name	1
hospital	4	neat	1
hour	4	need	6
house	1	never	4
hungry	5	new	9
husband	4	nice	12
		November	9
important	6	now	6
inside	10		
		okay	3
jerk	7	old	1
job	8	only	7
join	7	open	3
just	5	order	10
		over	3
kick	11		
kid	11	paper	1
kill	12	paperboy	9
kiss	11	park	3
kitchen	2	pay	6
knock	2	peace	12
know	4	people	1
		perfect	7
large	1	phone	4
last	7	play	5
late	4	please	6
lawn	1	policeman	3
leave	6	pull	3
left	5	put	7
lie	12		
life	5	question	3
light (*n*)	1	quiet	1
like	6		

read	6	study	5
really	3	stuff	10
record	9	stupid	9
refrigerator	5	supermarket	12
relax	10		
restaurant	1	table	11
right	5	talk	4
ring	4	tell	3
rob	12	think	4
room	2	time	5
run	5	tire	6
		today	2
sad	5	tooth (teeth)	7
Saturday	7	town	1
sauce	12	true	5
say	4	try	5
school	3	Tuesday	11
science	5	typical	3
second	9		
see (understand)	7	ugly	7
sell	9	under	11
shoe	3	understand	3
short	5	unusual	3
shot	12	upset	6
shrimp	5	usually	2
sign	10		
silent	1	walk	5
sit	6	want	3
sleep	3	warn	12
small	1	week	4
smartie	8	weekend	11
smile	8	white	1
some	3	widow	12
son	2	window	1
spaghetti	11	without	8
speak	6	woman	1
spend	9	wonder	4
stand	10	work	3
state	1	write	5
stay	9		
still	2	year	5
stitch	12	yell	3
stop	9	yesterday	8
store	1	yet	12
stove	11	young	7
strong	12		

Phrases

Chapter 1

the United States
gas station
be on
5:00 A.M.
be around
be closed
in the center of

Chapter 2

____ years old
be all over ____

Chapter 3

be in bed
make coffee
pull off
be the boss
Come on!
make a noise
be time to ____
have to
go to work
have school
Go away!
Stop it!
a lot (of)
be tired (of)
go back

Chapter 4

pick up
be hurt
police officer
10:00 P.M.
of course
be all right
Oh, (my) God.
be sorry
I'm afraid (that)
be with ____

Chapter 5

have (got) problems (with)
get to ____
be in class
be the matter (with)
make ____ feel better
screw up
all the time
be wrong (with) ____
do ____ right
What do you mean?
have a test
have a disease
be embarassing
have a ____ time
a little ____

Chapter 6

get ____ fixed
wait (for)
the way ____ look
have time (for) ____
All right.
Speak up.
What ____ for?
That's enough!
You've got to be kidding!
Let me think about it.
care about ____

Chapter 7

make an appointment
health club
be surprised
Come on.
spend time with ____
Oh, really?
Get out (of here).
go out
You're history!

Chapter 8

get mad (at)
Go ahead.
be to blame
what else
give ___ trouble
None of your business!
get sick

Chapter 9

paper route
lemonade stand
football team
get a job
in a way
get by
help out
have (got) a screw loose
find out ___
have a choice
get/be serious
be amazing
Get off my case!

Chapter 10

look ___ best
part-time job
full-time job
in front (of)
help wanted
fall (madly) in love
the ___ of ___ dreams
stuff ___self (with)
You're impossible.
That's all there is to it.
Who knows?
take a look (at)
be ready

Chapter 11

smile (about)
go on
Wait a minute.
deliver papers
the rest (of)
be settled

Chapter 12

spaghetti sauce
high school
be in love (with)
be crazy about ___
be married (to)
be divorced (from)
get together
say goodbye
be a dream
Come to think of it . . .